HEALING YOU

a journal for reflection

Jennie Liljefors

Illustrations by Mio Sallanto

murdoch books

Sydney | London

This book belongs to
_____
_____

contents

Preface

Most of us have something we need to process, heal or let go of. This notebook of tips, advice and exercises is a guide to help you find your way. It is designed to give you insight, tap into your internal state of being, charge your batteries and allow you to shine from the inside and out. The work we put into our mental, spiritual and physical development will help us grow.

Read, ponder, make notes, then put the book aside and look back through it at a later date. Reading through what you have written, uninterrupted and in a flow, can be enlightening and can give you an indication of how you really feel and what you can do to experience more harmony.

'Take root to rise' is a beautiful motto. It describes how we must begin by digging deep and becoming friends with the darkness we bear inside of us, so it does not stand in the way of our flowering. By seeing parallels in nature, where beauty is often born in darkness, we find we can more easily honour our own darkness. Think of the lotus flower with its roots in the mud and its beauty on the surface of the water.

An important part of the healing process is breaking your silence and sharing your story. I hope this book can help you achieve that.

I wish you the best of luck with your in-depth investment in yourself. And remember — you can always begin anew. It does not matter what happened earlier in your life, your spiritual development can start now.

Jennie Liljefors

How to use this book

As you work through this notebook, make time for reflection, use a pen you like, find a cosy space to write, and allow yourself to ignore your inner critic, letting the text flow freely without judging it. Remember that you are writing to get in touch with your own unique energy, your strength and your inner peace. The more you work to find your inner peace, the more you will discover how things fall into place. Writing helps us in our spiritual development.

Before you sit down with your notebook, take a moment to remind yourself of all that is good around you. Gratitude is an important part of our inner healing.

Send a message to the universe that you are ready for a change. By visualising what is important to you and expressing it in writing, you will be manifesting your energy and helping to make it happen. Write down your truth and magic will occur.

- This is my truth:

Crystals

To help amplify your feelings, learn more about crystals and work with them. Have your crystals out in front of you when you write, in your pocket during the day, in your hand during meditation or under the pillow while you sleep. Below is a selection of crystals that are beautiful to work with, along with a description of what each represents.

- Amethyst – a purple quartz that helps with spiritual development and enhances your intuition.
- Aventurine – a green quartz that enhances material and emotional wellbeing.
- Carnelian – an orange-brown gemstone that helps eliminate blockages and gives inspiration.
- Citrine – a golden brown quartz that gives happiness and peace.
- Malachite – a green semiprecious stone that brings joy and success.
- Turquoise – a blue-green stone that symbolises protection, strength and wellbeing.
- Rose quartz – a milky rose-coloured mineral that gives clarity and strength, and helps when you are distressed.

Essential oils

Essential oils are natural, beneficial substances that have been used for healing since ancient times. The scent of the oils helps to awaken and unlock trapped emotions; they are able to heal as well as calm you when you are stressed. You can add a drop to a glass of water and drink it, take a drop under the tongue, rub it onto your foot or wrist, or dab it behind your ear. Pour a few drops into the bath, use it in an aroma lamp (oil diffuser) or even add it to your body lotion. Here is a short list of some oils and their beneficial effects.

- Bergamot, jasmine – to calm the mind.
- Citrus varieties, peppermint – for more energy.
- Rosemary, cedar – for focus.
- Lavender, chamomile, frankincense (olibanum) – for calm, or better sleep.

The day y begin my
spiritual practice y feed
my inner light, which will
become stronger the more y
dedicate myself to it

Healing you

How can my inner light become stronger?

Sometimes we have to stop and ask ourselves, 'am I living a balanced life?' Negative patterns and difficult situations often leave traces of imbalance in our mental states or physical bodies. It is not strange or wrong, but these imbalances can be dealt with once they are observed and detected, helping to improve our lives.

We are often better at pushing imbalances away, even becoming accustomed to feeling less than good, rather than working through what has happened to us and what may still be affecting us.

Exercise

Close your eyes and breathe deeply. Do you feel any imbalance and, if so, where do you feel it? Write it down without reflecting or judging.

I take small steps towards healing

You can break a negative pattern with simple tools to help you find your sanctuary. Begin by giving yourself time, practise better breathing and mindfulness and work out physical tension through yoga, mantras and mudras. With these tools you can become more receptive to love and forgiveness. You can increase your courage and strength, which will boost your self-confidence. Improved health also makes it easier to follow the flow of life, in both its ups and downs.

● What do I need more or less of to feel better?

I accept my feelings and try to accommodate them

You may experience joy and happiness, but also sorrow, anger and resistance during your practice, and afterwards in your writing. Accept your feelings and see if you can accommodate them.

When you have finished an exercise, ground yourself by lying down and resting with a warm blanket over your body. It helps you reflect and lets the insights you have gained land within you.

Writing things down can teach you a lot about yourself, because you can go back and reread your notes.

● Feelings I am dealing with now:

....

....

....

....

....

....

....

....

*I let go of
the burden I carry*

A good way to get out of any vicious circle is to write about the difficult situation you have been in, or continue to be in. Writing about it and then reading back over what you've written can help you understand it from a different perspective.

Exercise

Close your eyes and take deep, calm breaths. On a piece of paper, describe the incident you were in, or the situation you still find yourself in. Then create a ritual to release yourself from this problem. When you have finished writing, set the paper alight and let it burn in a fireproof dish. Let it burn out. Be still and focused. Decide that when the paper is all burnt, your problem can no longer disturb you. If you want, you can repeat the Sanskrit mantra *svāhā* to yourself, which roughly translates to 'I let go of the burden I carry'. Repeat this exercise as often as you like and whenever you like. Write down your thoughts afterwards.

what is my deep intention — my sankalpa?

Find your *sankalpa* for healing and spiritual development

An important part of your spiritual development involves getting in touch with your deepest intention of how you really want to live your life — this is called your *sankalpa*. With a clearer intention, you can more easily experience who you really are, instead of 'walking beside yourself' and watching your life rush past.

Exercise

Sit comfortably, close your eyes, breathe calmly and feel the vibrations in your body. Ask yourself, 'what do I want?'

Take time to listen. Write down what comes up without changing, judging or evaluating it. End the exercise and rest. Read the answers at a later date.

I open myself to the flow

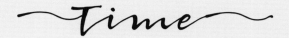

Time

Have you ever thought about what time really is? Time is relative, invented by humans to give ourselves a system, but the only thing we know about time is the felt presence of immediate experience, the place we find ourselves in right now. This is the moment for us to be aware and experience.

With tools such as breathing, mindfulness, meditation and yoga, we can gain proximity to the present moment: the now.

My thoughts on time:

_____

_____

_____

_____

_____

_____

_____

_____

_____

_____

_____

_____

I will give myself time every day from now on

Reflect on your time

Exercise

Sit still with your eyes closed and breathe calmly. Ask yourself,
'how much time do I give myself for doing what I wish to do,
and for my spiritual development? How much or how little
do I prioritise time for myself?'

- Make a note of your thoughts without judging them.

It is not the length
of my practice that matters
but its continuity

Find time for yourself each day. Get up earlier each morning for a week and do the exercise below when your energy is higher. Quietening your thoughts is an important part of getting in touch with your true self, and can prevent stress and fatigue.

Exercise

Snooze meditation. Instead of pressing the snooze button when your alarm goes off, sit up in bed, stretch, close your eyes, and quieten your thoughts by focusing on your breath. Sit still for at least 10 minutes. This will help centre you for the day.

● Write down how this morning routine has affected your week.

_____

_____

_____

_____

_____

_____

_____

to make room for
something new

When you give yourself a little more space over a period of time, you begin to perceive what is important to you and what you can discard.

● How can I find more time?

....

....

....

....

● What would I do if I had more time?

....

....

....

....

....

....

breathing and life force

Our bodies, like all life in the universe, share the same life force. The amount of life force our bodies possess is usually constant, but can fluctuate, becoming more or less strong.

Life force is conveyed through our breathing. Since breathing is affected by how we feel, it often becomes light and superficial when we are stressed or not feeling well, which results in our life force becoming weaker.

By doing breathing exercises, we learn to take deeper breaths to strengthen our life force while simultaneously reducing stress.

There is a saying that our lives have a certain number of allotted breaths — therefore, by taking deeper breaths, we are in a way extending our lives.

Tip!

Begin each morning with deep, calm breaths. Do the same before sleeping. If you wake up during the night and cannot get back to sleep, try taking deep breaths and, in your mind, follow the breath in and out of your body.

y soften
with my breathing

Natural breathing

Many of us are not conscious of our own breathing. Making a journey of discovery into our natural breathing is a way to help us understand how we are really feeling.

Give yourself a moment every day to sit or lie in a comfortable position and just observe your natural breathing. Breathe in and out through your nose and focus on the space under your nostrils where your breath comes in and out. Notice the pause between the breaths. Putting all expectations aside, just feel it. Attention to breathing, apart from invoking a sense of calm, gives you the many benefits of breathing through your nose. The body's oxygenation improves, the mucous membranes of the nose and throat decongest and the air is more effectively filtered.

Exercise

Count how many natural breaths you take in one minute. Write down the number of breaths without judging. Repeat this exercise whenever you do your breathing practice and note down the result.

ﾂ inhale
new soothing energy
ﾂ exhale
worry and stress

Conscious breathing

Once you become more familiar with your natural breathing, you can start practising conscious breathing. During the inhalation, begin to deepen the breath in your stomach and allow your chest to expand in all directions. Hold one hand on your stomach and one hand on your heart as reference points. Focus on your breath, following it with your mind, in and out of your body. Let go of thoughts and allow your breathing to become meditative.

Gradually, you can begin to extend your breath by lengthening the exhalations. When it feels good, you can also inhale for longer. Then practise having equally long inhalations and exhalations.

Exercise

Practise conscious breathing for one week. Once more, count how many natural breaths you take in one minute. Reflect and write down how your breath training has affected you.

Drops of stillness — collect deep-breathing minutes

Once you have improved your breathing through practice, stop for a break once an hour, close your eyes and breathe deeply. At the end of the day, you may have collected a quarter of an hour's worth of deep-breathing minutes — I call them drops of stillness.

Exercise

Reflect on how valuable these minutes are for you. Write down your thoughts as they come to you while you breathe deeply; these words can provide valuable inspiration. Also, reflect on how your daily drops of stillness affect you.

*...let go, relax
and rest quietly to receive
the healing power of nature*

How do you sleep?

For better and more restful sleep, breathe deep, calm breaths when you go to bed. If you wake up in the middle of the night, you can do the same exercise instead of tossing and turning.

Exercise

For one week, practise breathing deeply at bedtime and write down each morning how you have slept and what you have dreamt.

The bridge between
the heart and the mind
is my breath

We can easily tell how we feel and get in touch with our souls by paying attention to our breathing. By becoming more aware of our breathing, we open up an inner treasure chest that contains our truth, our innate wealth.

Exercise

Observe how you breathe in various situations throughout one day and write it down.

y let my thoughts quieten
and my mind rest

mindfulness and meditation

Mindfulness and meditation can help us calm our minds by quietening rushing thoughts. We become more mindful and find it easier to be in the present.

These practices offer a much-deserved break from everyday life, with its constant stream of new information and new impressions. They give us the opportunity to turn inward and feel our moods, rather than directing all our attention outward, which we often do when busy and socialising. The entire body is positively affected by deeper breathing and we become both more relaxed and more focused. There are various techniques we can use, such as focusing on breathing, on a mantra or a mudra. The main thing is that we only observe what comes up in the form of thoughts and bodily sensations without shifting our focus. We allow ourselves to be where we are, with what is. We do our practice without judging or valuing.

Remember!

When practising mindfulness and meditation, breathing can often become almost superficial. At times it may feel as if you are barely breathing. This is nothing to be afraid of; you will get the air you need. It is a natural step in the process of quietening down.

I am here for myself
I am filled with peace,
love and harmony

Try doing this mindfulness exercise every day for a week.

Exercise

Sit in a comfortable position. Stretch your entire spine, focus your gaze on a fixed point, then close your eyelids and keep your eyes still. You can also try to gently turn your inner gaze up towards your third eye — the space between your eyebrows, your intuitive centre. Begin taking deep, soothing breaths, preferably emitting some long sighs as you exhale through your mouth. Then switch to just breathing through your nose. Relax your jaw and release your tongue from the palate. Relax your temples and the space between your eyebrows. Focus on breathing. If thoughts arise, let them come but also pass; return your attention to breathing.

Enjoy your breathing. It is intimate and sensual to sit close to oneself and one's breath. You will surely feel moved when you soften and go within. Let any thoughts come up; do not push away your emotions, but just continue with your breathing.

Become aware of your feelings and accept them just as they are. Can you see beyond them to get in touch with your inner self?

● Write down thoughts, feelings and images that arise during the exercise, and also how you feel afterwards.

I regain hope and trust

With a regular mindfulness practice, you will have the opportunity to get in touch with your truth, to learn to appreciate the small things in your everyday life and to come closer to peace in your soul and heart. Try focusing your mindfulness with the exercise below.

Exercise

Use your mindfulness practice to reflect on three good things about your day and write them down.

Tip!

You can also do this exercise by talking with a friend, your partner or your children.

*I release myself
from obstacles*

A mindfulness practice can create much-needed distance from negative and destructive thoughts that can block us. Thoughts are not facts or truths, but only inner perceptions that pass by. If we notice how a thought springs up, we can also understand how it loses its power. With this insight we can learn to recognise which thoughts are based on truth and which are not, and from there continue on to action.

Realising that we do not have to act on every thought is the beginning of learning to live with what we have been through — or are dealing with now — with dignity, instead of judgement. If one fights against bad thoughts, they will only grow, and the suffering will increase.

Exercise

Do this exercise to free yourself from identifying with your thoughts. Begin your mindfulness practice as on page 53. When negative thoughts come up, try to see them with the benefit of wisdom. Remind yourself that this is just a thought. Recall that you are not your thought, nor the feeling it gives you, and therefore you do not need to act on it. Notice what is happening in your consciousness and in your body.

Conclude the exercise when you feel you want to by breathing a few deep sighs. Open your eyes and rest for a while. Write down any insights you have had.

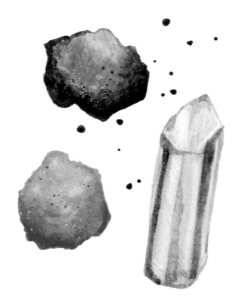

y take in what is

Mindfulness and meditation can help you see the bigger picture and give you a feeling of being part of it. You will find it easier to accept the flow of life — whether in happiness or sorrow, in success or adversity — without harbouring feelings of reluctance or needing to change what comes to you.

Exercise

Write down how you handle everyday challenging situations as you practise mindfulness.

I
open up
to my
inner
strength

Love and kindness meditation

Exercise

Begin your mindfulness practice as on page 53. Repeat the
following phrases silently or out loud to yourself, with love from
your innermost being to yourself, and then follow the exercise.
This exercise can be difficult to do, especially when it is directed
at someone you are in conflict with. You may be thinking negative
thoughts; let the emotions come, but continue the practice. Feel
how your words radiate with your energy.

- **To yourself**

  May I be healthy and happy.

  May I live in peace, love and harmony.

- **To someone you know**

  May you be healthy and happy.

  May you live in peace, love and harmony.

- **To someone you do not know, but meet in your
  everyday life**

  May you be healthy and happy.

  May you live in peace, love and harmony.

- **To someone you are in conflict with**

  May you be healthy and happy.

  May you live in peace, love and harmony.

- **To all people on Earth**

  May we all be healthy and happy.

  May we all live in peace, love and harmony.

  Then visualise that you are filled with feelings of wellbeing, happiness, peace, love, harmony, goodness. Experience being filled with the meaning of these words, their power beaming out from within you. Carry this power with you.

- Write down what comes to you: feelings, thoughts, sensations.

. . . .

. . . .

. . . .

. . . .

. . . .

. . . .

If you can breathe
you can do yoga

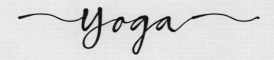

Yoga

The physical side of yoga gives us softer, stronger and more resilient bodies and more flexible and supple spines. By applying ourselves to yoga, we can free ourselves from muscular blockages, quieten our thoughts and release ourselves from any accumulated tension in our entire being.

Yoga suits everyone. If you can breathe, you can do yoga. Yoga meets us wherever we may find ourselves in life: at whatever age or lifestyle we have, whether we are healthy or sick, stiff or flexible. We do not have to be in any particular condition to practise yoga. We just have to be who we are.

Exercise
Lie on your back. Breathe deeply. Stretch and flex your entire body and then relax. Inhale while raising a knee up to your chest and hold it with both hands. Leave the other leg as straight as possible on the floor. Exhale as you release. Then repeat with the other leg. This releases tension and fatigue in the lower back.

● Write down the feelings that occur during and after the exercise.

. . . .

. . . .

. . . .

y get a new perspective

Yoga is an effective tool to help us heal on a spiritual level if we have experienced something difficult. With yoga, it can be very liberating to find that we do not have to focus on the negative *per se*, but more on the effects that still reside in the body, such as tension, pain and breathing difficulties.

Exercise

Lie on your back with your legs bent and your feet wide apart. Let your arms stretch out to the sides, palms facing up. While exhaling, lower both knees to the right, leaving your feet on the floor. If you want to deepen the rotation, place your right foot on the outside of your left knee and allow your legs to rest against the floor. Then turn your chest to the left. Hold this position for a while. Change sides.

   This is a simple exercise that rotates the spine, releasing tension and deepening breathing. These twists help you see things from new perspectives. Do this exercise for a few days in a row and write down how it feels.

*I am softening
around my heart*

Yoga techniques help us learn to listen to our hearts, seek the light within us, and open up our inner worlds. Yoga helps us lower our stress levels and turn off our alarm systems. As our inner bodies become more radiant, softer and lighter, our physical bodies can relax more and feel less tension.

Yoga can help us heal body and mind so that we can regain control over our lives.

Exercise

Kneel on all fours. Inhale and arch your back slightly, lifting your head and sitting bones, then exhale and round your back up, pulling your chin in against your chest. Move gently between these two positions as you breathe. Also try doing circular movements with your upper body, even with your head and neck. Then rest with your bottom down on your heels and forehead against the floor in the child's position. Relax and breathe. Can you feel the tension subside?

I see my situation from
a different perspective

Yoga offers soft, accessible positions as opposed to the pressure, stress and perhaps violence we encounter in everyday life. We choose what position we want to do, how long we want to stay in it and when we want to end it. We gradually take control of muscles that have been blocked and strained. Then we can deepen our practice with due care and love.

Exercise

Note: do not do this exercise if you suffer from neck problems, have high blood pressure or heart problems, are menstruating or pregnant, or if you have eye problems, such as detached retina.

Lie on your back with your bottom slightly away from a wall and stretch your legs up against the wall. Relax your legs and let your arms lie so they feel comfortable. Hold this position for up to 10 minutes, then bend your legs and turn onto your right side.

    This exercise increases circulation in the pelvis, abdomen, heart and head. It relieves tired legs, swollen feet and back pain and helps with insomnia, while also providing energy. It is a universal position that is said to rejuvenate your entire system and help you see things from a different perspective.

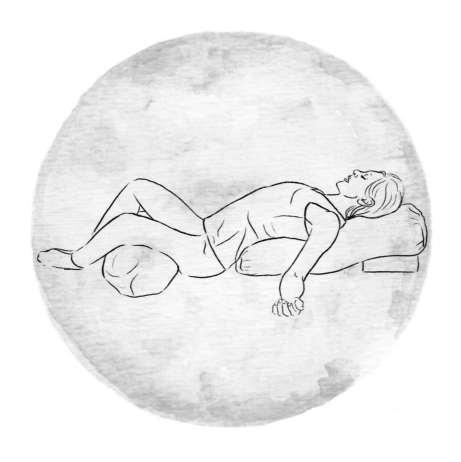

y recover and find new balance

Restoratative yoga involves resting in various positions, which is something everyone can do. You are mindful in a state of wakefulness, which provides a different form of rest than when you sleep. Should you happen to find yourself in a state of physical or mental pain, stress, hopelessness, sadness, illness or in need of rehabilitation, this calm yoga is wonderful and healing.

At first you may feel extreme fatigue, but your energy will return. Taking time to rest and relax every day is important for a more balanced life and helps eliminate stress-related illnesses, cure their side effects and prevent stress from becoming chronic.

Exercise

Lie on your back with pillows under your back and head, letting your head rest higher than the rest of your body. Place pillows under your knees and let your knees bend and fall to the sides, allowing the soles of your feet to meet. Let your arms rest with your hands slightly raised on small pillows or on the floor. Breathe and rest for as long as it feels good to you.

Challenge yourself to do some restorative yoga every day for a period of time. Write down how it feels when you give yourself time to rest on a daily basis.

I rest in myself
I am here for myself

Yoga is also a guide to how we can live our lives and take care of ourselves and our surroundings. It guides us to be honest, humble, kind-hearted and helpful.

With our yoga practice, we have the tools to stay on track in challenging situations and to change that which is niggling inside of us. As yogis, we can more easily see the lesson to be learnt in each challenging situation we encounter.

Exercise

Let yoga become a daily routine for a period of time. Do some exercises in breathing, mindfulness or a physical position every day. Write down how it affects you.

I look within

Here are some questions you can ask yourself regarding your own practice:

- Am I being honest with myself?

....

....

....

- How can I be more honest with myself?

....

....

....

- Three things I appreciate about myself:

....

....

....

om namah shivaya
Ham sa
aum

y unlock myself
to find a new flow

Mantra

A mantra is a word that has a specific meaning. It is a tool for letting go of thoughts so we can become more mindful. In the philosophy of yoga there are countless mantras that are written in Sanskrit. Each mantra carries a complex understanding of how its syllables encapsulate energies that pulsate within us and produce vibrations that affect the body and mind in a positive way.

   You repeat the mantra silently to yourself or out loud. You can even sing the mantra, which is called chanting. Through repetition, the mantra becomes one with our inner selves, assimilated and experienced. The more we use a mantra, the more powerful it becomes.

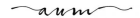

aum

One of the most common mantras, also said to be the original mantra and one that represents the divine, is *aum* (or *om*). One interpretation is that the entire universe was created as a result of the resonance that emerged after *aum*, with the letters of the word standing for creation and rebirth, for sustaining and preserving and for dissolution and ending.

Everything in our environment has the same cycle. Everything is created, maintained and then dissolved in an eternal circle. By reciting the mantra of *aum*, one becomes aware of one's own part in evolution.

You can also use *aum* to focus on what you need help with right now. Maybe something new needs to be born, or you just need to stay strong in what is, or you need to bring something to an end.

Exercise

Recite the mantra *aum* silently or loudly on each inhalation and exhalation as you practise mindfulness or meditation. Continue for as long as it feels good. When you have finished, sit and rest a little while in the vibrations of the mantra.

● Write down any thoughts, feelings or emotions that arise.

. . . .

. . . .

. . . .

. . . .

hamsa

The mantra of *haṃsa* (or *soham*) means 'I am that', with 'that' meaning pure consciousness. This mantra should remind us that our true self is pure consciousness. It is called the 'natural mantra' or 'the mantra of the breath', because it resembles the sound that is made by a breath passing through the nostrils.

Exercise

Practise thinking or reciting *haṃ* when inhaling and *sa* while exhaling. Try to synchronise the mantra with your breathing.

Write down your thoughts and feelings.

Om namaḥ shivāya translates approximately as, 'I bow to the divine, which is my true self'. It is a healing mantra that helps you to feel, experience, understand and honour your true and innermost self.

Exercise

Chant this mantra every day for a period of time before going to sleep, or when you feel anxious or fearful.

● Write down your thoughts.

....

....

....

....

....

....

....

....

Mudra

Mudrā is Sanskrit for 'gesture'. There are many kinds of mudras. Some are expressed using the entire body, as when we do positions in yoga, while others are practised just using hand gestures.

With hand mudras the fingers are placed in specific positions. This helps to awaken the life force via nerve impulses, and we guide the life force to stay within our body instead of flowing out through our fingers. By using energy channels and energy centres, we can control the direction of life force in our body.

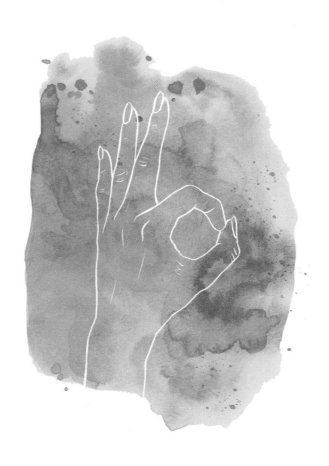

*I am in touch
with my truth
and my wisdom*

Gyana mudra & Jñana mudra

These mudras are usually done during breathing exercises or during mindfulness or meditation practice. They are for unifying the conscious self (thumb) with our innate wisdom (index finger). We can turn our palms down to face the earth to gain power (*gyana mudrā*) or up to the sky to show that we are open and ready for the next step (*jñana mudrā*). These mudras stimulate our parasympathetic nervous systems and lower the stress levels in our bodies.

Exercise

Let your thumb and forefinger meet with very light pressure. The other fingers are straight without being tense.

Try to feel what effect the mudra is having on you. Write down what you perceive after each session.

. . . .

. . . .

. . . .

. . . .

. . . .

. . . .

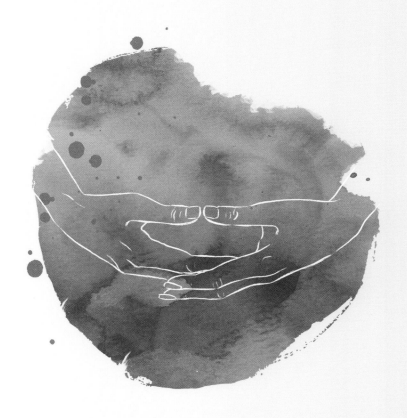

y am finding peace

Dhyana mudra

This mudra is helpful when you practise mindfulness and meditation. It is also a pose many of us naturally and unconsciously make when we sit still for a while or want to rest. This mudra calms the mind, promotes healing, balances the left and right sides of the body and increases concentration.

Exercise

Let both hands rest in your lap. The palms face upwards with the right hand on the left. The tops of the thumbs meet.

Try to feel what effect the mudra is having on you. Write down what you perceive each time after doing it.

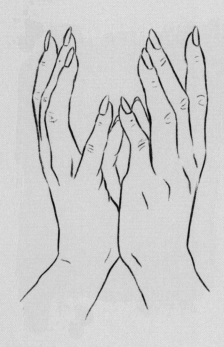

y am pure
y am light
y am genuine

Lotus mudra

The lotus mudra is inspired by the beauty of the lotus flower, a flower that floats on the surface of the water with its splendour open to the sky and its roots submerged in the mud. This mudra symbolises that light and beauty can emerge from darkness. It reminds us of our ever-present inner light and beauty, and calms our minds.

Exercise

Let the palms of your hands meet, spreading your forefinger, middle and ring fingers like a lotus flower blossoming. Keep the base of your palms, thumbs and little fingers in contact. Focus on your breathing. Imagine breathing in a warmth that fills you with love and awakens your inner beauty. Exhale your burdens. Observe what arises within you without judgement. Sit for as long as it feels good.

   Try to feel what effect the mudra is having on you. Write down what you perceive after each time you do it.

*y find stillness and
feel close to my heart*

love

During and after difficult events in life, it is common to carry
negative emotions that can create obstacles to loving ourselves
and thus prevent us from flourishing and living the life we desire.
This can lead to a retreat into solitude with a heavy heart.

In order to heal, we must begin by opening our hearts and
finding our way back to love and to a belief in ourselves. Yoga,
mindfulness and meditation can help us develop and deepen
this self-love.

Exercise

Focus on physically softening as well as strengthening the area
around the heart, shoulders, shoulder blades and chest where
many blockages occur. Arch and twist your back, as these exercises
are uplifting for the soul and help us to process the past. Accepting
what you have been through is a big part of the healing process.

Lie on your back, placing some pillows so that your back softly
arches. Have your head rest at the same height as your back or tilt
it slightly back for a deeper arch. Gently stretch the front of your
body and open up the space around your heart.

I open my heart

Exercise

In order to draw closer to your heart's desire, ask yourself
this question.

● Am I following my heart's desire or am I going in the direction
others wish me to go?

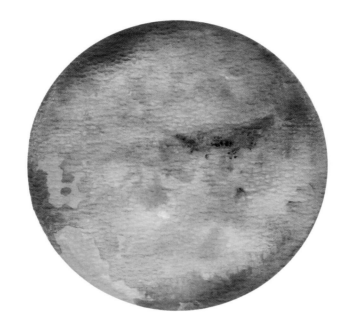

I let everything go and welcome new energy

Forgiveness

During and after difficult events in life, it is common to harbour feelings of aggression, guilt and vengefulness. Withholding forgiveness is like slowly being torn apart from the inside. Working with forgiveness in our practice can help us to be free in our hearts. What has happened has happened, and the more dark feelings we have, the heavier our hearts will be. Offering forgiveness is a way to move on. It does not mean that we accept or push aside what has happened to us, just that we do not allow it to take up any more space and energy in our lives.

Exercise

One mantra to use for forgiveness is *svāhā*, which roughly means that we do our best and we let go of the rest. Try to use this mantra in your mindfulness and meditation.

- Write down your reflections.

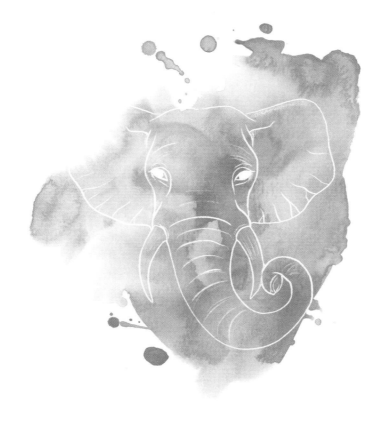

*I summon
and connect with all
my inner strength*

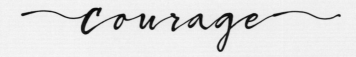

courage

Our courage is cultivated in our hearts. With a closed and broken heart, it becomes harder to be brave. We can heal by first addressing our hearts with love and forgiveness and then practising courage by getting in touch with our inner strength.

If we have been threatened or frightened, it is common to suffer from fear, big or small, that prevents us from living fully. With yoga we can use our bodies to tap into our inner potential, invigorating our strength and courage. Practising balance and inverted poses helps us reinforce and reach our full inner strength and potential.

Exercise

Before and during your yoga practice, ask yourself these brave questions.

● What do I want in my life?

. . . .

. . . .

● How do I want to live my life?

. . . .

. . . .

may y be without fear
may y find inner strength

Abhaya mudra — for courage and peace

In your mindfulness and meditation practice, use *abhaya mudrā* to gain a sense of inner security, to sit in peace with courage and in the absence of fear. Use this powerful mudra to dare to feel love when life is hard, and when fear, hatred or anger consume your energy.

Exercise

Hold up your right hand at shoulder height with an open palm facing outward and your fingers pointing upwards. Let your left hand rest on your left knee and form a circle with your thumb and forefinger. Imagine that you are breathing in golden light that fills you with courage and that you breathe out all your obstacles.

   Observe what thoughts arise inside of you and do not judge them. Stay seated for as long as it feels good.

● Write down your thoughts.

y turn upside down
for new strength
and new perspective

strength

Turning our bodies upside down gives them new strength and provides new perspectives on life. An inspiring mantra for practising the increase of mental and physical strength is *pūrṇa*, which more or less translates as 'complete' and implies that we are complete just as we are — like the moon, which is always full, even when only a small part of it is visible.

We should stop every now and then and let our bodies talk to us. We have an entire mechanical system that functions without us even having to think about it.

We have inexhaustible elemental power and strength. Sometimes we run so fast towards new goals that we get stuck in old habits, or get locked in by things that have happened and forget about our inner strength.

Exercise

Stop and remind yourself of everything that works within you. Write down your words.

*lift the corners
of your mouth up
into a smile*

Good health

We are able to contribute significantly to our own good health. Often this is by small, simple everyday changes. One small but powerful trick is to smile. When we smile, we send out signals to our bodies that we are feeling well. Try to smile for a few days during your practice and exercises and even as you write.

● What effects do smiles have on you?

A good idea is to start each day by scraping your tongue with a tongue scraper. Then brush your teeth and, ideally, use dental floss. Caring for one's mouth, teeth and gums is an important part of good health.

Drink a glass of lukewarm water, preferably with a drop of essential oil that suits you for the day (see suggestions on page 13). A couple of times a week, you can start the day with lemon water to cleanse your intestines.

● Write down the effects you feel when you give yourself some dental care.

y recover and find new balance

Go out into nature every day, as nature is healing in and of itself. Look up into the sky. Discover the forest, sea and earth.

● Write down what you see and experience.

Be sure to drink at least three to four litres of water every day for one week.

- Write down what the effects are on your digestion, sleep, concentration and skin.

Eat organic food as often as possible. Try to eat a lot of fruit and vegetables. When you help prepare your plate of food, think about quality before quantity, and beauty above all. Eat fresh ingredients, locally produced, if possible.

● Write down how you feel after you have eaten.

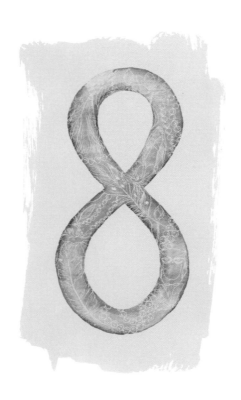

Epilogue

The final word is not mine but yours.

Finish your journey through this book by writing down your new beginning. Or let it be the start of your journey if, like me, you sometimes start working your way through a book back to front.

Write down your USP — your unique selling point. What makes you unique? Refrain from making comparisons to others, or thinking that others are better. Bring out the unique, remarkable and amazing you instead.

Before you begin, take this book, a pen and something that smells good and appeals to you, such as a fresh lemon, a drop of lavender oil or a beautiful flower. Also, take something from nature, such as a lovely stone, a seashell or something else that comes from the earth. Put your chosen objects in front of you and within easy reach.

Do some nice stretches, fill your lungs with oxygen and exhale some deep sighs. Then sit down in a comfortable position, take one of the objects in your hands, close your eyes and take in its scent with some deep breaths. Fill your senses. Raise a smile. Then repeat silently to yourself:

- I am unique.

- I am ready to let the uniqueness within me blossom more and more.

- No-one on Earth shall make me feel inferior without my consent.

Let the following affirmations sink in and settle down. When you feel ready, start by writing down (there is plenty of space on the next page):

- Three things you like about yourself.
- Three things you want to develop in yourself.
- Three things you want more of in your life.

Then select one of each of the above and form a sentence.

Example

'I think I am brave. I want to develop my passion for writing. I want spend more time in nature.'

Now convert the sentence to your USP.

Example

'I am a brave person with a passion for writing and an ability to see the magic of nature.'

Write this sentence on a sticky note and put it someplace visible, have it as a screensaver on your computer, or as a reminder on your phone. Let this sentence become your mantra.

Good luck with your exercises, and remember: you deserve to travel your own path. If the path you travel is not the path of your heart, it is not the right one.

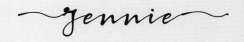

● Three things I like about myself:

....

....

● Three things I want to develop in myself:

....

....

● Three things I want more of in my life:

....

....

● Now choose one from each of the three points above
and compose your USP:

....

....

....

....

Published in 2021 by Murdoch Books, an imprint of Allen & Unwin
First published in 2019 by The Book Affair, Sweden

Murdoch Books Australia
83 Alexander Street
Crows Nest NSW 2065
Phone: +61 (0) 2 8425 0100
murdochbooks.com.au
info@murdochbooks.com.au

Murdoch Books UK
Ormond House
26–27 Boswell Street
London WC1N 3JZ
Phone: +44 (0) 20 8785 5995
murdochbooks.co.uk
info@murdochbooks.co.uk

For corporate orders & custom publishing, contact our business development team at
salesenquiries@murdochbooks.com.au

Illustrations © Mio Sallanto
Designer and project manager: Gabriella Sahlin

Publisher: Corinne Roberts
Translated by Richard Sexton

Text © Jennie Liljefors 2019

ISBN 978 1 92235 158 6 Australia
ISBN 978 1 91166 823 7 UK

A catalogue record for this
book is available from the
National Library of Australia

A catalogue record for this book is available from the British Library

Printed by C & C Offset Printing Co. Ltd., China

MIX
Paper from
responsible sources
FSC® C008047

The paper in this book is FSC® certified.
FSC® promotes environmentally responsible,
socially beneficial and economically viable
management of the world's forests.